OTHER BLACKBIRDS

ALEX JOSEPHY

I0191526

CinnamonPress

INDEPENDENT INNOVATIVE INTERNATIONAL

Published by Cinnamon Press
Meirion House,
Glan yr afon,
Tanygrisiau
Blaenau Ffestiniog,
Gwynedd, LL41 3SU
www.cinnamonpress.com

The right of Alex Josephy to be identified as author of this work has been asserted by her in accordance with the Copyright, Designs and Patent Act, 1988. Copyright © 2016 Alex Josephy.
ISBN: 978-1-910836-07-1

British Library Cataloguing in Publication Data. A CIP record for this book can be obtained from the British Library.

Designed and typeset in Palatino by Cinnamon Press.
Cover design by Jan Fortune.
Printed in Poland

Cinnamon Press is represented in the UK by Inpress Ltd and in Wales by the Welsh Books Council

Acknowledgments

I would like to thank Robert Vas Dias and Myra Schneider of the Poetry School for constructive criticism and inspiration over many years; Chris Considine for her careful and encouraging mentoring; and David Hornbrook, who makes me breakfast and puts up with the constant presence of other blackbirds.

Poems in this collection first appeared in the following publications: 'The Sister-Brother Treaty' and 'Marias' won joint first prize in the Battered Moons poetry competition, 2013, 'A Slip of Wilderness' appeared in *Artemis* 6, May 2011; 'Assembly' appeared in *Obsessed with Pipework*, Autumn 2009; 'The Only Meal I Ever Saw my Father Cook' appeared in *London Grip* (online), June 2009; 'Joy' appeared in *The Rialto* 56, November 2004, and in *Images of Women*, Arrowhead press, 2006; 'Elbows on the Table' appeared in the anthology *In Terra Pax*, Cinnamon Press, 2011; 'Notwithstanding' was very highly commended in the *RSPB/Rialto* nature poetry competition, 2013; 'Semaphore' appeared in the *Poetic Republic* anthology, 2013; 'La Macchia' appeared in *The Clearing* (online), December 2014; 'Scalandrino' won the McLellan poetry prize, 2014; 'Bless This Woman' appeared as 'Red Sky' in *Domestic Cherry*, January 2013

Contents

Other Blackbirds

The Sister-Brother Treaty

The sun for you, the moon for me.
Easy. On the verandah we drew

our map of the universe, breathing
the vanilla scent of wooden slats

in sunshine. You laid claim to all the fields
of England; forests were mine, Ashbrook

to Transylvania. Viaducts went to you
and steam, steam in the engines

and the bathrooms and the boilings
of kettles. I took river bridges, fords,

surprised you with teapots. You threw in
eels, watercress beds, then snatched spiders

and the Suez Canal, lifted on the spur
of the moment from the buzz that teased

our ears, drifting through the French doors
from the wireless on the dresser,

two shiny knobs beyond my reach.
Our treaty signed, sealed, indelible

as the name-tapes sown inside
our Aertex shirts, while the adults mumbled,

rattled china, moved about their business
in the shadow-land indoors.

Give Them Back

words deleted from the Oxford Junior Dictionary, 2007

acorn, adder, ash, beech, bluebell, buttercup

words that rhymed with the woods, your muddy boots,
my coat specked with skeleton leaves, ripped on briars;
secret passwords; crossed sticks in the copses

catkin, conker, cowslip, cygnet, dandelion

treasures spied through timothy grass, knees green,
fingers yellow; latticed shell, leaking earth that stank
of dead snail; owl pellets hoarded in your pocket

fern, hazel, heather, heron, ivy, kingfisher, lark

lemony bite of sorrel stalk, lit reeds we passed
between us for cigarettes; prickle of nettle-rash
up my arm; you cured it with a dock leaf

mistletoe, nectar, newt, otter, pasture, willow

that big-leafed plant we'd never seen before
whose name we invented: Purple Lugubrious;
nouns you helped me hoist from the brook
in a jam jar, verbs that crawled from a chrysalis

A Slip of Wilderness

I swayed there, held in forest light
      all through summer, gave them the slip
so easily. Grocer's van in the lane,

low-flying swans; I was away
      into the rough boughs of the yew,
smearing my palms with dust

that clung like soot. I'd climb
      through all its brittle bannisters
up to the tree's dry, secret heart,

greenfinch-watching far above
      the unbearable lawn, breakfast,
lunch, tea. Could sway there still,

live once again close to the sky, wrapped
      in a leaf curtain, a sea-green needle cloth
sewn with deep red berries, each

cupping its poison seed. Touch
      the tip of my tongue to one, crush one
down the skirt of my party frock.

Assembly

Introducing Mozart,
one eyebrow raised, lips pursed,
Miss lowers the needle;

Fran twitches next to me,
touches a septic ear,
head bent as if in submission.

Silence, dust, dry crack of vinyl,
then a far-away piano. The hall fills up
with cherry-pink Cremola Foam.

Our trick's taking effect;
torn blotting paper
stuffed into my lace-up shoes

is pulling the blood to my feet
till I am faint, just as Fran said,
dizzy. This waltz

swings me around,
multiplies me by three,
feathers my neck.

I focus on the girl in front
hair twisted into a blonde plait
that holds the world in place.

Captive

You explore my palm with curious lips
whose upper ledge, prehensile
like the bud of an elephant's trunk
can clutch at grass stalks, paint
dewy circles on skin. Your nostrils test
what's lately been in my pocket,
in my mind, on the wind. Tilt
one horn foot, let me trace the lie
of rough gold hairs along your neck
and each swivelling ear, softer,
warmer than a silk purse.

You bend your head willingly
to the halter, yet I can't trust you
to stay; I've sketched a square
with wire and wooden posts
to keep you near: portrait horse
in a landscape. But this paddock
is no prairie; when rain strikes,
you plume your tail, uneasy.
Go then, roll your eyes, show me
how you can pound the earth to scuds,
sail clear over the fence.

The Only Meal I Ever Saw My Father Cook

Stink of burnt white bread
he'd scrape with a whirring bone-handled knife,
black flakes snowing into the chickenfeed bucket.

Eggs fried lacy, fat flipped over yolks till they dulled,
blind eyes on a china plate, and rashers with the rinds on
curled like red-and-white party ribbons.

Spit and billow of steam when he doused the pan
under the cold tap. Oily gobbets
fizzed on the tiles, blown Catherine wheels.

At the siege of Tobruk, a miracle:
dehydrated cauliflower scavenged from the harbour
blossoming in a mess tin filled with salt water.

Give it a rest, our mother groaned.

And in his eighties, alone in the bungalow
at six a.m., no-one to please or irritate,
beetroot sandwiches were all he wanted,

monumental slabs of bloomer and beet,
eaten with purple fingers at the cold kitchen table,
no knife, no fork, no fuss.

Post Prandial

Sunday after lunch in the bar, the uncles frown;
they need this estuary, this bluster of wind.
Storm and tide will rearrange what's scattered
on the pebbles, strew salted bottletops,
ferry away the skeletons of black-skinned eels
we grilled Saturday night. These aunts
I've never met before; they drink like gulls,
all beak. Waves imitate the way they kiss,
sway of their hips. The red flag's out; high wind
blows an uncle down the jetty, furls him
in his greatcoat. We carry him indoors,
pull apart the buttons. Inside he's cuttle white.

No chance of an afternoon nap. The table's laid
with two-pronged forks, every inch of the spotted cloth
alert. Sit tight, the parents hiss. Time for a game
of boil, slice, tea and cake. On the far shore
through steamed-up window glass, a boatmen's shed,
hazy, hard to make out. We should visit
another year, the aunts insist. Pale smoke
meanders from a chimney over there
as if on their stove they were brewing snow.

What She Wants

at the Green Gate, 1983

She saw what she wanted
tied to the razor wire
with red satin ribbon
between a wilting rose
and a peace sign: Crystal Barbie,
the doll I wouldn't buy
not even for Christmas

and while we sang, argued
with the young constable, posed
for the photo-journalist, she ran
to claim her prize, eleven inches
high, beamed from another world:
hair floss, pearlised bodice,
changeling princess feet.

A Language

My daughter thrives
on chlorine air, glances back

as we pass mid-lane, flips
with a seal's tweak

at the turn. My hands sketch
water-boatman circles,

frog legs thrust
an afterthought.

She's on her back
twenty metres down-pool,

ducks underwater just to spin
to the surface, refracted

into Cubist slivers. Lycra. Legs.
Bubble stream. Double-helix

becoming a girl.
Those articulate limbs,

what they're capable
of imagining! She arrows

for the deep end; I tread water,
watch each clean stroke

replaced, improved on
by the one that follows.

Icon

My desktop paperweight's this clay head,
unglazed, circa 1988, unsigned.
It crouches, glum eyes, wide nostrils,

on half-completed this and that,
the unanswered, the unpaid,
the illegible, photocopies

and flimsies; holds them still.
With scratch moustache
and gouge ears, once supplied

with pinched-out flaps, vestigial
as Venus de Milo's arms,
it grows wiser, more mysterious

as the years pass. There's a shine
to the cheeks where I've held it
in my palm, grey Yorick, stroked it

with my thumb. A kitchen fork
made the rough comb-over
that decorates the crown.

I know the maker: Jamie,
and the subject: his grandpa.
It's now the sole survivor

of an evolutionary chain:
from walking-head studies of me
to Miss Kettle with horrid frown,

to winged skateboards (after Leonardo),
portraits of Battle-Cat. It makes me smile
and cover my laughter, just as I did

the end-of-term Friday before Christmas
when he carried it home, Scotch-taped
in bubble-wrap, clutched in both mittened hands.

Joy

It's June, it's hot, it's raining
and you've shorn off
nearly all your hair,
dyed the rest black,
and you're my child.
We've been at this bus stop
for over half an hour,
cars surfing past, stirring a brew
from blocked gutters
to chuck up at our feet

and yet the air's still sweet
as apricots, the Late-Nite shop
is open, and your father's girl
has given you a leather jacket
once owned, she says,
by Tony Curtis's wife,
and even though you're fifteen
and I don't for one moment
imagine you'll have noticed,
you're holding my hand.

Elbows on the Table

The room is cold, butter hard
in the dish, and they have on
heavy jumpers. He's deep
in history: Tuscany, 1945,
a gatehouse blown to pieces
in the long retreat. He turns down
a corner, worries a crease
close to the spine, breadcrumbs
cinder-light in the fold.

Her elbow nudging his,
she's landed in another age;
in her head she's a pirate's child
at the court of the Virgin Queen.
She loves this story: a parterre
of branching paths. She hops
between the box hedges,
picks a sprig of rosemary, reads
the last paragraph first,
then Chapter Two: white moths
flutter between her palms.

Coffee cools in the chipped enamel jug.
Slices of toast stand in the rack:
unturned pages. He looks up,
looks through her, smiles,
frowns, picks up his glasses.

Armadio

It's different in Italian;
>taller, a heart full of air,
any number of arms,
>eyes, buttonholes.
Coat-hangers tangle
>in the gloamy interior;
their triangle music
>inaudible from outside
thrills the rail,
>an overture. Oak panels
hold the breath
>of gauzy evenings,
metamorphosis in silk,
>cool white cotton.
Four seasons rub shoulders,
>gripped in the purgatory
of last year's lavender.

Sheet Lightning

It photographs
thin air, glancing down

through ghosts of olive trees,
startled stones in the road,

everything implicated,
no source, no destination,

you and me in the green Suzuki
glow-worm bright. Electric skeins

brush but seem not to touch
what they illuminate

so that the town itself
from this distance crackles awake,

wavers, burns down to black.
The Sat Nav scrolls, deletes,

searches for satellites.
Home could be anywhere.

Asylum

The vaporetto wallows past
another island; we crowd at the rail,

holding out phones to catch
the view. Skeleton trees loopy with ivy

shield demented ghosts, plague pits.
A loggia sags in a scaffold cage.

They say the soil's half earth,
half human ash. A fishing net is spread

over a wall to dry. A plastic chair
abandoned in a bramble patch

looks out to sea. Such places,
with their cruel histories, preserve

a kind of wilderness. Someone
has landed a small boat,

somebody's marked the wall.
And isn't that a plume of smoke,

beyond the bell-tower? Maybe
they imagine a future here, hiding out

in this fragment of the past. But in our wake,
speculators raise their binoculars;

an evening breeze sweeps
the lagoon, feels like an eviction.

Notwithstanding

your elderberry eyes; the sleek line of your back; your fawn pelt; the way you ripple when I move near; your creamy underside; your habit of sitting bolt upright, moving your head to and fro; the sheen on your delicate claws that still clutch a morsel of pecorino cheese; your rounded ears that light up in the sun, and the optimistic curve of your tail; your ceaseless and methodical gnawing, one wire after another, again and again, never for a moment giving up hope; notwithstanding any and all of these,

after nightfall you will be taken from this house, shaken from this cage, decanted onto the North slope of the hill, left to find your own way onward under the moon, through the tall stalks of grass, docks and thistles.

Semaphore

She never says a word.
It's on the line, the washing line
that circulates two wobbly pulleys;
she creaks it out each morning
through third-floor shutters.

It goes around, it comes around
like sushi on a moving belt,
precious and side-dishes,
the sweet, the sour. Four socks.
A pause. Two pairs of boxer shorts.

A sagging pillow case. A football top.
An orange summer dress, printed
with sunflowers. A white blouse
full of breeze, all the buttons missing.
Silence; the line rattles and jerks,

then a ripped shirt. Seven dishcloths,
wet as drowned rats hung by the tail
and then— beyond all help —
a plait of long dark hair
tied with a green ribbon.

Scheletri

two they found
she told me
oh Madonna
under upheaved stones
of the chapel floor, the year
they began the renovation
now abandoned for lack of funds
the town's need for a squash court
roof-beams left to warp
banners to bleach
nailed door

        she couldn't say
        what became of them
        whether lowered by
        hard-handed wall-makers
        back to the hollow place
        painted with fumes
        of their distillation
        grinning side-by-side
        since the long siege broke
        when Medici stamped his crest
        high on the gatehouse arch

                or evicted, crushed into sacks
                Dio, Heaven help us
                as bones eventually are
                to leave room
                for incumbents
                the young generation
                of the dead
                carried to the ossuary
                the commune of bones

                shelved; after all these years
                raised one or two inches
                closer to paradise

After tomorrow

Crais, prescrai, pescrille, pescruflo, maruflo, maruflone, maruflicchio
old Lucanian words for tomorrow, and the day after, and the days after that

Crais
you will find yourself on a train,
windows smeared with the blur of hills,
school kids winged with luminous backpacks
chirping up and down the carriages.

Prescrai
drinking espresso at the airport
you will recall Chiara, the young *parrucchiera*
with dark brown eyes, who twisted your hair,
reamed it into rough blond terraces.

Pescrille
you will get up late in London, find the jacket
you wore all winter, pull from a pocket
two plump chestnuts. They'll wink
in your hand, still sleek as good leather.

Pescruflo
will be a wraith, it will remind you
of mornings with Chiara when a fine mist
rode up the ravine, a soundless cavalry,
to dissipate above the bell tower.

Maruflo
day of fury. You will curse the bus,
the Tube, the turnstile queue. Everyone
will be arguing. Nothing will rhyme.
Tomorrow and tomorrow you will still be here.

Maruflone
is unpredictable. The sky could be virgin blue;
she may phone. You may find words to write.
'*Crais*' may become all you need to know,
the word for tomorrow, or for never.

Maruflicchio:
this one's inevitable. It will come in the form
of those November biscuits, the Bones of the Dead,
hard as stones in the fields of Lucania
baked by her grandmother to last through till the
spring.

A Restoration

Who is that woman with the two ducks
strapped to the top of her hat?
A basket of eggs, such a timid frown.
I've knelt close on folded sheets
for a fortnight, mending holes in her gown
with a fine white filler, edged

my narrow brush across her cheek.
As if she's a lover or child, she needs
my kiss, but salt obscures her lip,
mottles the words she tries to mouth
in efflorescence. Here in the faintest slip
of lampblack, her cottage

hides among pines. All day I scrape
blown mortar, soothe hail-stone scores
with a spatula. Hills at her shoulder
wobble, *terre verte, verdegris.* Hands
reach and fail, lost in a fall of plaster,
caput mortuum, browned purple

at her feet. This is the lost treasure —
woman, duck hat, dancing dog — if only
I can give them back their shadowy journey
close to the bare earth, terra cotta, umber,
far from tin-leaf haloes, the well-worn story
told in cinnabar, shell gold, peach-stone charcoal.

Burnt

Love, you're a sunflower, one in a crowd
all saluting the sun, heads cranked to taste

the last of September. Your heart's a dial turned
to seed, a child's windmill stalled, out of order. Stand,

brandish your poor leaves streaked and spotted, catch
what you can to sustain you through the days

beyond yellow. Shake out the percussion of husk-set,
sap-sink, petal-fall. Shiver in after-gold, feel it

wither your rags, your wrecked corona, flame on flame
on flame, the whole field lifted on the blaze.

Garden of Herbs and Poisons

To walk in the *ortus cinctus*,
circular garden, touch the sunshine
stored in redbrick walls, consoles me
like nothing else these cloudy days.

Ajuga reptans, bugle, herb of San Lorenzo, a herb to soothe many ills,
a sore head from drinking or any broken bone.

When nothing changes,
        no letter comes, addressed
in your familiar script,

        I watch the basil grow,
schiudersi, one day
        then another,
stay close
        when it breaks
the soil, raises
        slender arms to the sun,
shaking free
        its bitter green banners.

Taragon, *dragoncello*, little dragon from Siberia, for snakebite
or a nagging tooth.

Days when the mirror shows a crone,
        when boredom or arthritis
slow my steps, eyelids sag
        with the weight of years,

I forget gloves, dig in the earth
      with bare hands, crush
the sodden crumbs of light
      and water, coat my fingers
with slippery clay, the white *crete,*
      unearth ridged stone, discover under my palm
the cracked, beautiful face of the hillside.

Atropa Mandragora, mandrake, a twist of contradictions: aphrodisiac,
anaesthetic, drives you mad, then if it hasn't killed you, dulls the pain.

Marias

Baby Maria long-awaited, garlanded
in lace, enthroned and bawling
in a wide black pram.

Maria, our Virgin of Humility gowned in blue
settled on the ground with baby Jesus
in a car park full of angels.

Maria in the corner shop, cutting ham
into pink petals in the slicer.

Maria Lady of Succour
who saved the town from invasion.

Wild Maria of the torrent
who lives on her own.

Terra cotta Maria in a niche
above the iron-work shop;
her calm, cracked smile runnelled with rain.

Crazy Maria, zucchini buds
in her hair.

Silent Maria in the shadows
of her shrine; offerings of dried grass,
cross-bow arrows, jar
of wood anemones, a football scarf.

Scabby Maria sent home
for fighting in the playground.

Miraculous Maria of the Snowballs
in August.

Easter Maria in a back room
at the *Comune*, waiting for the electrician
to mend her fairy-light halo.

Maria named in a poster
on the wall by Sant' Egidio,
departed this life last week, loved
and missed by her family, a photo
from the 1980s framed in black.

La Macchia

this forest is no fairytale

trackless, the heart hidden, it rips
        your sleeve

holm oak, tree heath, myrtle and juniper
        tangle with spurge olive, strawberry tree
            sage, blackthorn, mastic,
                broom

        oaks stud themselves with corky galls
ragged woody blooms, bark petals

acorn rug winds on ahead,
        amplifies each footfall

easy to lose your way
        look back
            it fills in fast behind

        remember
that tree with a scar the shape
of a half-open eye

        trunk with a splay
        of parallel harp strings

      the blue-feathered hollow
where foxes dined on jay

      the charcoal burners knew this place
        camped on frozen ground through winter
      tending the slow crimp of wood
into brittle sticks, their black fortune

and who knows which fugitives lay low
                              in speckled shadow
                round their own banked fires

dazzle of glade
and dusty green illegible thicket

Scalandrino

Wishbone-curved, it hangs
between forks and hoes in the lean-to.

He made it from the split trunk
of a chestnut sapling, not for the farm

but the small field near the house
where the children splashed in a trough,

hot July afternoons. Made it slender,
carved the top like a prow, to slide

into the crook between two boughs,
each rung narrower than the last

as he ascended through curled leaves,
wasps, breaks of sky. He'd straddle the frame,

fill a basket to the brim; cherries
for the sour-sweet jam they liked

more than anything. These days, it's rare
he'll venture to the orchard. One son's

a bank clerk, one's in California. Hard
to come by now, these *scalandrini*; might

be worth a bit, if anyone remembered
the shack overgrown with vines,

the ladder, bone-dry, silvering
in the dark among the onion-wreaths.

Other Blackbirds

The nest among the vines
by my back door was on the verge
of maiden flights, the day you phoned
and I visited Siena. Nothing
to do with you (how could it be?)

or the child, the one you're carrying
or imagining. Nor was the crown
of upturned beaks, their watery cries,
nor the amber-eyed tabby
that kept returning to the garden wall.

At Buonconvento, other birds carolled
in a cypress thicket; I waited
on cracked concrete. One bird flashed
across the tracks, sharp orange beak
dripping with worms

and I thought about Adlestrop,
English railway sandwiches, tea,
and how those fledglings soon will scatter,
how soon I'll lose sight of them
among all the blackbirds in Italy.

Bless This Woman

She taught me how to fly
       saying think of it as impro,
nothing but a gorgeous raid
       on gravity's drag,
the implausibility
       of flight. Above all,
put on lipstick, Tango Red.

Don't rely on a good send-off
       or a seat at the front,
or who sits next to you.
       Don't expect to hold hands.
Bend with the horizon,
       let it scroll. Fixate
if fix is what you need,

on curves: follow
       the starburst shapes of cities,
join dots between ships.
       Hold your own hand.
Ask yourself: when did a wing
       ever fall from a bird?
Smile in Vermilion. Don't eat

the dried ham roll, or count
       the cost, the damage leaked
across the stratosphere.Think
       of the plane's kind face,
the metal gills, the herring lips
       guzzling plankton
in a Paul Klee ocean. Don't

look down at your feet,
        or at the sardine can
they're resting on. Drink gin
        and make this turbulence
a drum solo that lasts too long
        but all you'll remember
is the bravura swirl

that rolls in at the end
        and you'll applaud,
 all of you glad when you tumble
        into the canyon
of descent, houses, motorway,
        footlights, landing strip,
and on your lips, Sky Red.

www.ingramcontent.com/pod-product-compliance
Lightning Source LLC
Chambersburg PA
CBHW020956030426
42339CB00005B/130